Delicious

crumbles
&
cobblers

Delicious
crumbles
&
cobblers

LOVE FOOD

This edition published in 2009 for Index Books Ltd

Love Food ® is an imprint of Parragon Books Ltd

Parragon
Queen Street House
4 Queen Street
Bath BA1 1HE, UK

Introduction, cover text, and new recipes by Lorraine Turner
Photography by Don Last
Home economy by Christine France

ISBN 978-1-4075-1626-4

Printed in China

Notes for the reader

• This book uses metric and imperial measurements. Follow the same units of measurements throughout; do not mix imperial and metric.
• All spoon measurements are level: teaspoons are assumed to be 5 ml and tablespoons are assumed to be 15 ml.
• Unless otherwise stated, milk is assumed to be low fat and eggs are medium. The times given are an approximate guide only.
• Some recipes contain nuts. If you are allergic to nuts you should avoid using them and any products containing nuts. Recipes using raw or very lightly cooked eggs should be avoided by infants, the elderly, pregnant women, convalescents and anyone suffering from illness.

Contents

Crumbles and cobblers have been around for a long time, but what exactly is the difference between them? Are there any tips for ensuring a perfect dish every time?

According to some food historians, crumbles and cobblers both originated from the pie. The pie itself can be traced back through many centuries, to the time of the ancient Egyptians. They used a primitive form of bread dough to enclose fruits and nuts, which were sweetened with honey. However, it was the ancient Greeks who first started to make pastry with flour and water, and used it to enclose different meats. Eventually the ancient Romans adopted the pie, and later it spread to Europe.

Since then, the pie has spread around the world and has undergone many transformations, with each nation or culture adapting it to suit the circumstances and food availability of the time.

The difference between a crumble and a cobbler is that, whereas a crumble is topped with a thin, crunchy layer, a cobbler is usually topped with a thicker layer of scones. A cobbler can be either savoury or sweet. In a savoury cobbler the bottom layer will contain meat, fish, beans, vegetables, or a mixture of these: the topping will consist of plain or cheese-flavoured scones, or scones that have been flavoured with fiery or savoury spices such as chilli or paprika. In a sweet cobbler, the bottom layer will contain fruits, nuts, honey and/or chocolate: the topping will comprise sweet plain scones or scones that have added ingredients such as sweet spices or dried fruits.

The crumble became widely popular in Britain as a result of the strict food rationing that took place during the two World Wars in the first half of the 20th century. Thrifty cooks used the crumble topping – a mixture of flour, sugar and unsalted butter – as an economical replacement for

traditional sweet pastry. It needed smaller quantities of the key ingredients used to make pastry, which were scarce at the time. Its flexibility was also an attraction, because it could be used as a topping for any fruits that happened to be available at the time.

The sugar in the crumble topping caramelises while it is baking, creating a deliciously sweet and crunchy topping that contrasts well with the tartness of different fruits. It also pairs beautifully with chocolate and sweeteners such as honey and maple syrup. The sweetness of the topping means that sweet crumble recipes, such as fruit and chocolate, are more common, but it is also possible to make a savoury version by replacing the sugar in the topping with something else, such as nuts. The Mixed Bean & Vegetable Crumble in this book is one such example, and will delight crumble enthusiasts and vegetarians alike.

This book has irresistible crumble recipes for every occasion and, alongside innovative dishes such as the savoury crumble, you will find some well-known favourites such as Apple & Blackberry Crumble, and Rhubarb Crumble.

Within these pages you will find some delicious cobbler recipes, from traditional favourites such as Beef Cobbler with Chilli or Golden Chicken Cobbler, to innovative new interpretations on this timeless dish, such as Strawberry Cream Tea Cobbler, a wonderful reinvention of the great British cream tea. Or why not try the Chocolate Cherry Crumble with Cranberries & Port, a delicious dessert to warm and inspire you during Christmas or chilly winter nights?

The Classics

serves 4

900 g/2 lb cooking apples, peeled and sliced

300 g/10½ oz blackberries, fresh or frozen

55 g/2 oz light muscovado sugar

1 tsp ground cinnamon

crumble topping

85 g/3 oz self-raising flour

85 g/3 oz plain wholemeal flour

115 g/4 oz unsalted butter

55 g/2 oz demerara sugar

single or double cream, to serve

apple & blackberry crumble

Preheat the oven to 190°C/375°F/Gas Mark 5.

Peel and core the apples and cut into chunks. Place in a bowl with the blackberries, muscovado sugar and cinnamon and mix together, then transfer to an ovenproof baking dish.

To make the crumble topping, sift the self-raising flour into a bowl and stir in the wholemeal flour. Add the unsalted butter and rub in with your fingers until the mixture resembles fine breadcrumbs. Stir in the demerara sugar.

Spread the crumble over the apples and bake in the preheated oven for 40–45 minutes, or until the apples are soft and the crumble is golden brown and crisp.

Serve hot with cream.

serves 6

900 g/2 lb rhubarb

115 g/4 oz caster sugar

grated rind and juice of
1 orange

crumble topping

225 g/8 oz plain or
wholemeal flour

115 g/4 oz unsalted butter

115 g/4 oz soft brown sugar

1 tsp ground ginger

cream, yogurt or custard,
to serve

rhubarb crumble

Preheat the oven to 190°C/375°F/Gas Mark 5.

Cut the rhubarb into 2.5-cm/1-inch lengths and place in a 1.7-litre/
3-pint ovenproof dish with the sugar and the orange rind and juice.

Make the crumble topping by placing the flour in a mixing bowl
and rubbing in the unsalted butter until the mixture resembles
breadcrumbs. Stir in the sugar and the ginger.

Spread the crumble evenly over the fruit and press down lightly using a
fork. Bake in the centre of the oven on a baking tray for 25–30 minutes
until the crumble is golden brown.

Serve warm with cream, yogurt or custard.

serves 6

125 g/4½ oz unsalted butter,
plus extra for greasing

175 g/6 oz brown sugar

500 g/1 lb 2 oz fresh apricots,
stoned and sliced

1 tsp ground cinnamon

crumble topping

175 g/6 oz wholemeal flour

50 g/1¾ oz hazelnuts, toasted
and finely chopped

fresh clotted cream, to serve

apricot crumble

Preheat the oven to 200°C/400°F/Gas Mark 6. Grease a 1.2-litre/
2-pint ovenproof dish with a little unsalted butter.

Put 3 tablespoons of the unsalted butter and 100 g/3½ oz of the
sugar in a saucepan and melt together, stirring, over a low heat.
Add the apricots and cinnamon, cover the saucepan and simmer
for 5 minutes.

To make the crumble topping, put the flour in a bowl and rub in
the remaining unsalted butter. Stir in the remaining sugar and
then the hazelnuts.

Remove the fruit from the heat and arrange in the bottom of
the prepared dish. Sprinkle the crumble topping evenly over the
fruit until it is covered all over. Transfer to the preheated oven
and bake for about 25 minutes until golden.

Serve hot with fresh clotted cream.

serves 6

500 g/1 lb 2 oz rhubarb

500 g/1 lb 2 oz cooking apples

grated rind and juice of
1 orange

½–1 tsp ground cinnamon

85 g/3 oz light soft brown
sugar

crumble topping

225 g/8 oz plain flour

125 g/4½ oz unsalted butter
or margarine

125 g/4½ oz light brown
sugar

40–55 g/1½–2 oz toasted
chopped hazelnuts

2 tbsp demerara sugar
(optional)

rhubarb & orange crumble

Preheat the oven to 200°C/400°F/Gas Mark 6. Cut the rhubarb into 2.5-cm/1-inch lengths and place in a large saucepan.

Peel, core and slice the apples and add to the rhubarb, together with the grated orange rind and juice. Bring to the boil, lower the heat and simmer for 2–3 minutes until the fruit softens.

Add the cinnamon and sugar to taste and turn the mixture into an ovenproof dish, so it is not more than two-thirds full.

Sift the flour into a bowl and rub in the unsalted butter or margarine until the mixture resembles fine breadcrumbs (this can be done by hand or in a food processor). Stir in the sugar, followed by the nuts.

Spoon the crumble mixture evenly over the fruit in the dish and lightly smooth the top. Sprinkle with demerara sugar, if liked.

Cook in the preheated oven for 30–40 minutes until the topping is browned. Serve hot or cold.

serves 4

4 apples, peeled, cored and diced

5 plums, halved, stoned and quartered

4 tbsp fresh apple juice

25 g/1 oz soft light brown sugar

crumble topping

115 g/4 oz plain flour

75 g/2¾ oz unsalted butter, diced

25 g/1 oz buckwheat flakes

25 g/1 oz rice flakes

25 g/1 oz sunflower seeds

50 g/1¾ oz light brown sugar

¼ tsp ground cinnamon

single or double cream, to serve

apple & plum crumble

Preheat the oven to 180°C/350°F/Gas Mark 4.

Mix the apples, plums, apple juice and sugar together in a 23-cm/9-inch round pie dish.

To make the crumble topping, sift the flour into a mixing bowl and rub in the unsalted butter with your fingertips until it resembles coarse breadcrumbs. Stir in the buckwheat and rice flakes, sunflower seeds, sugar and cinnamon, then spoon the topping over the fruit in the dish.

Bake the crumble in the preheated oven for 30–35 minutes, or until the topping is lightly browned and crisp. Serve with cream.

serves 4

4 large pears

crumble topping

115 g/4 oz self-raising flour

100 g/3½ oz unsalted butter, diced

5 tbsp demerara sugar

2 tbsp finely chopped hazelnuts

toffee

3 tbsp golden syrup

3 tbsp demerara sugar

2 tbsp unsalted butter

2 tbsp single cream

½ tsp vanilla extract

vanilla ice cream, to serve

pear & toffee crumble

Preheat the oven to 200°C/400°F/Gas Mark 6.

To make the crumble topping, put the flour in a large mixing bowl, then use your fingertips to rub in the unsalted butter until crumbly. Stir in 4 tablespoons of the sugar and the chopped hazelnuts, then cook in the preheated oven for 5–10 minutes until heated through.

To make the toffee, put the golden syrup into a saucepan over a low heat. Add the sugar, 1 tablespoon of the unsalted butter, and all the cream and vanilla extract, and bring gently to the boil. Simmer for 3 minutes, stirring constantly, then remove from the heat and set aside.

Put the remaining unsalted butter in a frying pan and melt over a low heat. Meanwhile, peel and roughly chop the pears, then add them to the pan and cook, stirring gently, for 3 minutes. Stir in the toffee and continue to cook, stirring, over a low heat for another 3 minutes.

Transfer the pear-and-toffee mixture to an ovenproof pie dish. Arrange the crumble evenly over the top, then sprinkle over the remaining sugar. Bake in the preheated oven for 25–30 minutes, or until the crumble is golden brown.

Serve hot with vanilla ice cream.

serves 4

6 nectarines

25 g/1 oz demerara sugar

2 tbsp sweet sherry

crumble topping

185 g/6½ oz plain flour

55 g/2 oz demerara sugar, plus
extra for sprinkling

100 g/3½ oz unsalted butter,
melted

crème fraîche, to serve

sherried nectarine crumble

Preheat the oven to 200°C/400°F/Gas Mark 6.

Using a sharp knife, halve the nectarines, remove and discard the stones, then cut the flesh into fairly thick slices. Put the nectarine slices into an ovenproof pie dish, sprinkle over the sugar and sweet sherry, and cook in the preheated oven for 5–10 minutes until heated through.

To make the crumble topping, put the flour and sugar in a large bowl, then quickly mix in the melted butter until crumbly. Carefully arrange the crumble over the nectarines in an even layer – keep your touch light or the crumble will sink into the filling and go mushy. Scatter a little more sugar over the top, then transfer to the preheated oven and bake for 25–30 minutes, or until the crumble topping is golden brown.

Serve hot with generous spoonfuls of crème fraîche.

serves 4

400 g/14 oz gooseberries

1 tbsp honey

85 g/3 oz caster sugar

1 tbsp orange juice

1 tbsp grated orange zest

6 tbsp water

thin strips of orange rind,
to decorate

crumble topping

115 g/4 oz self-raising flour

100 g/3½ oz unsalted butter,
diced

5 tbsp demerara sugar

50 g/1¾ oz pistachio nuts,
finely chopped

vanilla or orange-flavoured
ice cream, to serve

gooseberry & pistachio crumble

Preheat the oven to 200°C/400°F/Gas Mark 6.

Top and tail the gooseberries. Put them in an ovenproof pie
dish, pour over the honey and cook in the preheated oven for
5–10 minutes until heated through.

Put the caster sugar, orange juice, orange zest and water in a
small saucepan and bring to the boil, stirring, over a medium
heat. Reduce the heat and simmer for 5 minutes, then remove
from the heat and leave to cool.

Meanwhile, to make the crumble topping, put the flour in a
bowl, then use your fingertips to rub in the unsalted butter
until crumbly. Stir in 4 tablespoons of the demerara sugar and
pistachio nuts.

Pour the cooled orange syrup over the gooseberries, then lightly
sprinkle over the crumble mixture in an even layer. Do not press
the crumble into the syrup or it will become mushy. Sprinkle
over the remaining demerara sugar.

Bake in the preheated oven for 25–30 minutes or until the
crumble topping is golden brown. Remove from the oven,
decorate with strips of orange rind and serve with vanilla
or orange-flavoured ice cream.

serves 4

6 peaches

2 tbsp demerara sugar

2 tbsp orange juice

crumble topping

115 g/4 oz self-raising flour

100 g/3½ oz unsalted butter, diced

5 tbsp demerara sugar

3 tbsp finely chopped hazelnuts

single or double cream, to serve

peach & orange crumble

Preheat the oven to 200°C/400°F/Gas Mark 6.

Using a sharp knife, halve the peaches, remove and discard the stones, then cut the flesh into fairly thick slices. Put the peach slices into an ovenproof pie dish, sprinkle over the sugar and orange juice, then cook in the preheated oven for 5–10 minutes until heated through.

To make the crumble topping, put the flour in a large bowl, then use your fingertips to rub in the unsalted butter until crumbly. Stir in 4 tablespoons of the sugar and the hazelnuts.

Carefully arrange the crumble over the peaches in an even layer – keep your touch light or the crumble will sink into the filling and go mushy. Scatter the remaining sugar over the top, then transfer to the preheated oven and bake for 25–30 minutes, or until the crumble topping is golden brown.

Serve hot with cream.

serves 4

4 just-ripe bananas (not too ripe or they will be too mushy for this dish)

2 tbsp rum

fine strips of lime rind, to decorate

crumble topping

115 g/4 oz self-raising flour

zest of 1 lime, finely grated

100 g/3½ oz unsalted butter, diced

5 tbsp demerara sugar

50 g/1¾ oz desiccated coconut

vanilla ice cream, to serve

baked banana crumble with rum & lime

Preheat the oven to 200°C/400°F/Gas Mark 6.

To make the crumble topping, put the flour and grated lime zest in a bowl, then use your fingertips to rub in the unsalted butter until crumbly. Stir in 4 tablespoons of the demerara sugar and the desiccated coconut and set aside.

Slice the bananas lengthways and arrange them in an even layer in the bottom of an ovenproof pie dish. Pour over the rum, then lightly sprinkle over the crumble topping to cover the bananas. Do not press the mixture down or the bananas and crumble will go mushy. Sprinkle the remaining sugar over the top, then transfer to the preheated oven and bake for 20–25 minutes, or until the crumble is golden brown.

Remove from the oven, decorate with strips of lime rind and serve with vanilla ice cream.

Contemporary Twists

serves 4

6 tbsp unsalted butter
for greasing

400 g/14 oz canned apricots,
in natural juice

450 g/1 lb cooking apples,
peeled and thickly sliced

crumble topping

100 g/3½ oz plain flour

50 g/1¾ oz porridge oats

4 tbsp caster sugar

55 g/2 oz plain or milk
chocolate chips

single or double cream,
to serve

chocolate fruit crumble

Preheat the oven to 180°C/350°F/Gas Mark 4. Lightly grease an ovenproof dish with a little unsalted butter.

Drain the apricots, reserving 4 tablespoons of the juice. Place the apples and apricots in the prepared ovenproof dish with the reserved apricot juice and toss to mix.

To make the crumble topping, sift the flour into a mixing bowl. Cut the unsalted butter into small pieces and rub in with your fingertips until the mixture resembles fine breadcrumbs. Stir in the porridge oats, sugar and chocolate chips.

Sprinkle the crumble mixture over the apples and apricots and smooth the top lightly. Do not press the crumble into the fruit.

Bake in the preheated oven for 40–45 minutes or until the topping is golden.

Serve hot or cold with cream.

serves 4

2 mangoes, peeled and sliced

1 papaya, peeled, seeded and sliced

225 g/8 oz fresh pineapple, peeled, trimmed and cubed

1½ tsp ground ginger

100 g/3½ oz unsalted butter

100 g/3½ oz light brown sugar

crumble topping

175 g/6 oz plain flour

55 g/2 oz desiccated coconut, plus extra to decorate

tropical fruit crumble

Preheat the oven to 180°C/350°F/Gas Mark 4.

Place the fruit in a saucepan with ½ teaspoon of the ground ginger in a bowl, 2 of the unsalted butter and 4 tablespoons of the sugar. Cook over a low heat for 10 minutes until the fruit softens. Spoon the fruit into the bottom of a shallow ovenproof dish.

To make the crumble topping, combine the flour and remaining ginger in a new bowl. Rub in the remaining unsalted butter until the mixture resembles fine breadcrumbs. Stir in the remaining sugar and the coconut, then spoon over the fruit to cover completely.

Cook the crumble in the preheated oven for about 40 minutes or until the top is golden and crisp.

Decorate with a sprinkling of desiccated coconut and serve immediately.

serves 4

3 large, ripe cooking apples

3 large, ripe pears

1–2 tbsp lemon juice

60 g/2¼ oz unsalted butter

100 ml/3½ fl oz maple syrup

1 tsp almond extract

1 tsp almond-flavoured liqueur, such as Amaretto (optional)

whole or chopped almonds, to decorate

crumble topping

115 g/4 oz self-raising flour

100 g/3½ oz unsalted butter, diced

5 tbsp demerara sugar

50 g/1¾ oz almonds, finely chopped

clotted cream, to serve

caramelized apple & pear crumble

Preheat the oven to 190°C/375°F/Gas Mark 5.

Peel and core the apples and pears, then cut them into small chunks. Brush the chunks with a little lemon juice to prevent discoloration.

Melt the unsalted butter in a frying pan over a medium-low heat, add the apples and pears, maple syrup and almond extract, and almond liqueur if using. Cook the fruit for 5–7 minutes until softened, then remove from the heat and arrange the fruit and juices evenly in the bottom of an ovenproof pie dish.

Meanwhile, to make the crumble topping, put the flour in a bowl, then use your fingertips to rub in the unsalted butter until crumbly. Now stir in 4 tablespoons of the demerara sugar and the chopped almonds.

Lightly sprinkle the crumble mixture over the fruit in an even layer. Do not press the crumble into the syrup or it will become mushy. Sprinkle over the remaining demerara sugar and decorate with whole or chopped almonds.

Bake in the preheated oven for 20–25 minutes or until the crumble topping is golden brown. Remove from the oven and serve with clotted cream.

serves 4

crumble topping

115 g/4 oz self-raising flour

100 g/3 ½ oz unsalted butter, diced

5 tbsp demerara sugar

2 tbsp finely chopped mixed nuts

50 g/1¾ oz plain chocolate, finely chopped

filling

175 g/6 oz cherries, stoned

150 g/5½ oz cranberries

3 tbsp demerara sugar

6 tbsp port

halved cherries and/or whole cranberries, to decorate

double cream, whipped, to serve

chocolate cherry crumble with cranberries & port

Preheat the oven to 200°C/400°F/Gas Mark 6.

To make the crumble topping, put the flour in a large mixing bowl, then use your fingertips to rub in the unsalted butter, demerara sugar and the chopped mixed nuts, then stir in the chopped chocolate and set aside.

To make the filling, put the cherries, cranberries, sugar and port into a saucepan and stir gently over a low heat for 3 minutes. Transfer the fruit and juices to an ovenproof pie dish and sprinkle over the crumble topping. Scatter over the remaining sugar.

Bake in the preheated oven for 10–15 minutes, or until the crumble topping is golden brown. Remove from the oven, decorate with halved cherries and/or whole cranberries and serve with whipped cream.

makes 12

280 g/10 oz plain flour

2 tsp baking powder

¼ tsp bicarbonate of soda

¼ tsp salt

200 ml/7 fl oz milk

2 medium eggs

150 g/5½ oz unsalted butter, melted

115 g/4 oz fresh cranberries, roughly chopped

75 g/2¾ oz mixed nuts, chopped

200 g/7 oz demerara sugar

streusel topping

85 g/3 oz self-raising flour

1 tsp mixed spice

35 g/1¼ oz unsalted butter, diced

85 g/3 oz demerara sugar

4 tbsp chopped mixed nuts

cranberry streusel muffins

Preheat the oven to 190°C/375°F/Gas Mark 5. Line a 12-cup muffin tin with paper cases.

Sift the flour, baking powder, bicarbonate of soda and salt into a large mixing bowl. Make a well in the centre and add the milk, eggs and melted unsalted butter. Stir together gently until just combined. Do not overstir – the mixture should still be a little lumpy.

Add the cranberries, mixed nuts and demerara sugar, and again stir lightly, just enough to incorporate the fruit and nuts evenly into the batter. Distribute the batter evenly between the paper cases.

To make the streusel topping, put the flour and mixed spice in a bowl, then use your fingertips to rub in the unsalted butter until crumbly. Stir in the demerara sugar and the mixed nuts. At this stage you may need to add a little cold water to make the mixture stick together loosely.

Arrange the streusel topping on top of the muffins, then bake in the preheated oven for 20–25 minutes, until golden brown on top.

To test they are cooked, insert a cocktail stick into the centre of a muffin. If it comes out clean, the muffins are cooked. If not, return them to the oven for a few more minutes until cooked.

serves 4

crumble topping

115 g/4 oz self-raising flour

1 tbsp cocoa powder

5 tbsp dark muscovado sugar

2 tbsp finely chopped pecan nuts, plus extra to decorate

50 g/1¾ oz plain chocolate, finely chopped

filling

60 g/2¼ oz cocoa powder

250 ml/8 fl oz water

125 g/4½ oz caster sugar

2 tbsp unsalted butter, diced

4 large cooking apples

100 g/3½ oz unsalted butter, diced

deep chocolate crumble

Preheat the oven to 180°C/350°F/Gas Mark 4.

To make the crumble topping, put the flour and cocoa powder in a large mixing bowl, then use your fingertips to rub in the butter until crumbly. Stir in 4 tablespoons of the sugar and the chopped pecan nuts, then stir in the chopped chocolate and set aside.

To make the filling, put the cocoa powder, water and caster sugar in a small saucepan and cook, stirring, over a low heat for 3 minutes. Add the diced butter and return to a simmer, stirring constantly, then remove from the heat.

Peel and slice the apples, then spread them evenly in the bottom of an ovenproof pie dish (this has to be done quickly to prevent the apples discolouring). Warm them through in the oven for 5–10 minutes, then pour over half of the chocolate sauce and sprinkle over the crumble topping. Scatter over the remaining sugar and bake in the preheated oven for about 20–25 minutes, or until the crumble topping is cooked.

Just before the end of the cooking time, return the remaining chocolate sauce to the hob and warm gently. Remove the crumble from the oven, decorate with chopped pecan nuts, and serve with the warmed chocolate sauce.

serves 4

8 firm but ripe plums

25 g/1 oz demerara sugar

warm custard, to serve

crumble topping

185 g/6½ oz plain flour

55 g/2 oz demerara sugar,
plus extra for sprinkling

100 g/3½ oz unsalted butter,
melted

50 g/1¾ oz hazelnuts,
chopped

mini plum crumbles

Preheat the oven to 180°C/350°F/Gas Mark 4.

Using a sharp knife, halve the plums, remove and discard the stones, then cut the flesh into fairly thick slices. Divide the plum slices between 4 ovenproof ramekins, sprinkle over the sugar, then cook in the preheated oven for 5–10 minutes until heated through.

To make the crumble topping, put the flour and sugar in a large bowl, then mix in half the melted butter. Stir in the chopped nuts, then quickly mix in the remaining butter until crumbly. Carefully arrange the crumble over the plums in an even layer – keep your touch light or the crumble will sink into the filling and go mushy. Scatter a little more sugar over the top, then transfer to the preheated oven and bake for 25 minutes, or until the crumble topping is golden brown.

Serve hot with warm custard.

serves 8

pastry

175 g/6 oz plain flour

1 tsp baking powder

115 g/4 oz unsalted butter,
cut into small pieces

55 g/2 oz caster sugar

1 egg yolk

1–2 tsp cold water

filling

150 ml/5 fl oz double cream

150 ml/5 fl oz milk

225 g/8 oz plain chocolate,
chopped

2 eggs

crumble topping

115 g/4 oz light brown sugar

85 g/3 oz toasted pecan nuts

115 g/4 oz plain chocolate

85 g/3 oz amaretti biscuits

1 tsp cocoa powder

chocolate crumble pie

To make the pastry, sift the flour and baking powder into a large bowl. Rub in the butter and stir in the sugar, then add the egg and the water to bring the dough together. Turn the dough out and knead briefly. Wrap the dough and chill in the refrigerator for 30 minutes.

Preheat the oven to 190°C/375°F/Gas Mark 5.

Roll out the pastry and use it to line a 23-cm/9-inch loose-based flan tin. Prick the base with a fork. Line with baking paper, fill with baking beans and bake in the oven for 15 minutes. Remove the paper and beans. Reduce the oven temperature to 180°C/350°F/Gas Mark 4.

To make the filling, bring the cream and milk to the boil in a saucepan, remove from the heat and add the chocolate. Stir until melted and smooth. Beat the eggs and add to the chocolate mixture, mix well and pour into the pastry case. Bake for 15 minutes, remove from the oven and rest for 1 hour.

When you are ready to serve the pie, put the topping ingredients into the food processor and pulse to chop. If you do not have a food processor, put the sugar in a large bowl, chop the nuts and chocolate with a large knife and crush the biscuits, then add to the bowl with the cocoa and mix well. Sprinkle over the pie, then serve it in slices.

serves 6

1.8 kg/4 lb sweet pumpkin

pastry

55 g/2 oz cold unsalted butter, in small pieces, plus extra for greasing

140 g/5 oz plain flour, plus extra for dusting

¼ tsp baking powder

1½ tsp ground cinnamon

¾ tsp ground nutmeg

¾ tsp ground cloves

1 tsp salt

50 g/1¾ oz caster sugar

3 eggs

filling

400 ml/14 fl oz sweetened condensed milk

½ tsp vanilla essence

1 tbsp demerara sugar

streusel topping

2 tbsp plain flour

4 tbsp demerara sugar

1 tsp ground cinnamon

2 tbsp cold unsalted butter, in small pieces

75 g/2¾ oz shelled pecan nuts, chopped

75 g/2¾ oz shelled walnuts, chopped

sweet pumpkin pie

Preheat the oven to 190°C/375°F/Gas Mark 5. Halve the pumpkin and remove the seeds and the stringy insides. Put the pumpkin halves, face down, in a shallow baking tin and cover with foil. Bake in the preheated oven for 1½ hours, then remove from the oven and leave to cool. Scoop out the flesh and mash with a potato masher or purée it in a food processor. Drain away any excess liquid. Cover with clingfilm and chill until ready to use. It will keep for 3 days (or several months in a freezer).

To make the pastry, first grease a 23-cm/9-inch round pie dish with butter. Sift the flour and baking powder into a large bowl. Stir in ½ tsp cinnamon, ¼ tsp nutmeg, ¼ tsp cloves, ½ tsp salt and all the caster sugar. Rub in the butter with the fingertips until the mixture resembles fine breadcrumbs, then make a well in the centre. Lightly beat 1 egg and pour it into the well. Mix together with a wooden spoon, then use your hands to shape the dough into a ball. Place it on a clean work surface lightly dusted with flour, and roll out to a round large enough to line the pie dish. Use it to line the dish, then trim the edge. Cover with clingfilm and chill in the refrigerator for 30 minutes.

Preheat the oven to 220°C/425°F/Gas Mark 7. To make the filling, put the pumpkin purée in a large bowl, then stir in the condensed milk and the two remaining eggs. Add the remaining spices and salt, then stir in the vanilla essence and demerara sugar. Pour into the pastry case and bake for 15 minutes.

Meanwhile, to make the topping, combine the flour, sugar and cinnamon in a bowl, rub in the butter until crumbly, then stir in the nuts. Reduce the heat to 180°C/350°F/Gas Mark 4. Sprinkle the topping over the pie, then bake for a further 35 minutes. Serve hot or cold.

serves 4

1 large onion, peeled and chopped

125 g/4$^{1}/_{2}$ oz canned red kidney beans (drained weight)

125 g/4$^{1}/_{2}$ oz canned butter beans (drained weight)

125 g/4$^{1}/_{2}$ oz canned chickpeas (drained weight)

2 courgettes, roughly chopped

2 large carrots, roughly chopped

4 tomatoes, peeled and roughly chopped

2 sticks celery, trimmed and chopped

300 ml/10 fl oz vegetable stock

2 tbsp tomato purée

salt and pepper

crumble topping

85 g/3 oz wholemeal breadcrumbs

25 g/1 oz hazelnuts, very finely chopped

1 heaped tbsp chopped fresh parsley

115 g/4 oz cheddar cheese, grated

mixed bean & vegetable crumble

Preheat the oven to 180°C/350°F/Gas Mark 4.

Put the onion, kidney beans, butter beans, chickpeas, courgettes, carrots, tomatoes and celery in a large ovenproof dish. Mix together the stock and tomato purée and pour over the vegetables. Season to taste with salt and pepper. Transfer to the preheated oven and bake for 15 minutes.

Meanwhile, to make the crumble topping, put the breadcrumbs in a large bowl, add the hazelnuts, chopped parsley and grated cheese and mix together well.

Remove the vegetables from the oven and carefully sprinkle over the crumble topping. Do not press it down or it will sink into the vegetables and go mushy.

Return the crumble to the oven and bake for 30 minutes, or until the crumble topping is golden brown. Remove from the oven and serve hot.

Cobblers & Beyond

serves 6

900 g/2 lb fresh berries and
currants, such as blackberries,
blueberries, raspberries,
redcurrants and blackcurrants

85–115 g/3–4 oz caster sugar

2 tbsp cornflour

cobbler topping

200 g/7 oz plain flour

2 tsp baking powder

pinch of salt

55 g/2 oz unsalted butter,
diced and chilled

2 tbsp caster sugar

175 ml/6 fl oz buttermilk

1 tbsp demerara sugar

single or double cream,
to serve

fruit cobbler

Preheat the oven to 200°C/400°F/Gas Mark 6.

Pick over the fruit, mix with the caster sugar and cornflour and
put in a 25-cm/10-inch shallow, ovenproof dish.

To make the cobbler topping, sift the flour, baking powder and
salt into a large bowl. Rub in the unsalted butter until the mixture
resembles breadcrumbs, then stir in the caster sugar. Pour in the
buttermilk and mix to a soft dough.

Drop spoonfuls of the dough on top of the fruit roughly, so that
it doesn't completely cover the fruit. Sprinkle with the demerara
sugar and bake in the preheated oven for 25–30 minutes until the
crust is golden and the fruit is tender.

Remove from the oven and leave to stand for a few minutes before
serving with cream.

serves 4–6

6 peaches, peeled and sliced

4 tbsp caster sugar

$^1/_2$ tbsp lemon juice

$1^1/_2$ tsp cornflour

$^1/_2$ tsp almond or vanilla essence

cobbler topping

175 g/6 oz plain flour

115 g/4 oz caster sugar

$1^1/_2$ tsp baking powder

$^1/_2$ tsp salt

85 g/3 oz butter, diced

1 egg

5–6 tbsp milk

vanilla or butter pecan ice cream, to serve

peach cobbler

Preheat the oven to 220°C/425°F/Gas Mark 7.

Put the peaches into a 23-cm/9-inch square ovenproof dish that is also suitable for serving. Add the sugar, lemon juice, cornflour and almond essence and toss together. Bake the peaches in the preheated oven for 20 minutes.

Meanwhile, to make the cobbler topping, sift the flour, all but 2 tablespoons of the sugar, the baking powder and salt into a bowl. Rub in the butter with the fingertips until fine crumbs form. Combine the egg and 5 tablespoons of the milk in a jug and mix into the dry ingredients with a fork until a soft, sticky dough forms. If the dough seems dry, stir in the extra tablespoon of milk.

Reduce the oven temperature to 200°C/400°F/Gas Mark 6. Remove the peaches from the oven and drop spoonfuls of the topping over the surface, without smoothing. Sprinkle with the remaining sugar, return to the oven and bake for a further 15 minutes, or until the topping is golden brown and firm – the topping will spread as it cooks.

Serve hot or at room temperature with ice cream on the side.

serves 4

800 g/1 lb 12 oz strawberries,
hulled and halved

50 g/1¾ oz caster sugar

cobbler topping

200 g/7 oz self-raising flour,
plus extra for dusting

pinch of salt

3 tbsp butter

2 tbsp caster sugar

1 egg, beaten

25 g/1 oz sultanas

25 g/1 oz currants

about 5 tbsp milk, plus extra
for glazing

clotted cream, to serve

strawberry cream cobbler

Preheat the oven to 200°C/400°F/Gas Mark 6.

Arrange the strawberries evenly in the bottom of an ovenproof dish, then sprinkle over the sugar and cook in the preheated oven for 5–10 minutes until heated through.

Meanwhile, to make the cobbler topping, sift the flour and salt into a large mixing bowl. Rub in the butter until the mixture resembles fine breadcrumbs, then stir in the sugar. Add the beaten egg, then the sultanas and currants, and mix lightly until incorporated. Stir in enough of the milk to make a smooth dough. Transfer to a clean, lightly floured board, knead lightly, then roll out to a thickness of about 1 cm/½ inch. Cut out rounds using a 5-cm/2-inch biscuit cutter. Arrange the dough rounds over the strawberries, then brush the tops with a little milk.

Bake in the preheated oven for 25–30 minutes, or until the cobbler topping has risen and is lightly golden. Serve hot with clotted cream.

serves 4

4 peaches, halved and stoned

4 nectarines, halved and stoned

2 tbsp almond liqueur, such as Amaretto

50 g/1¾ oz caster sugar

cobbler topping

200 g/7 oz self-raising flour, plus extra for dusting

pinch of salt

3 tbsp butter

2 tbsp caster sugar

1 egg, beaten

about 5 tbsp milk, plus extra for glazing

25 g/1 oz flaked almonds

freshly whipped cream, to serve

peach & nectarine cobbler with almond liqueur

Preheat the oven to 200°C/400°F/Gas Mark 6.

Arrange the peaches and nectarines evenly in the bottom of an ovenproof dish, then sprinkle over the almond liqueur and the sugar and cook in the preheated oven for 5–10 minutes until heated through.

To make the cobbler topping, sift the flour and salt into a large mixing bowl. Rub in the butter until the mixture resembles fine breadcrumbs, then mix in the sugar, followed by the beaten egg. Stir in enough of the milk to make a smooth dough. Transfer to a clean, lightly floured board, knead lightly, then roll out to a thickness of about 1 cm/½ inch. Cut out rounds using a 5-cm/ 2-inch biscuit cutter. Arrange the dough rounds over the fruit, brush the tops with a little milk, then scatter over the flaked almonds.

Bake in the preheated oven for 25–30 minutes, or until the cobbler topping has risen and is lightly golden. Serve hot with cream.

serves 4

2 tbsp plain flour

4 skinless, boneless chicken breasts, cut into bite-sized chunks

2 tbsp butter

2 tbsp olive oil

1 large leek, trimmed and sliced

2 spring onions, trimmed and chopped

1 garlic clove, crushed

2 carrots, peeled and chopped

1 orange pepper, deseeded and chopped

1 tbsp tomato purée

1/2 tsp ground turmeric

200 ml/7 fl oz white wine

200 ml/7 fl oz chicken stock

1 bay leaf

salt and pepper

cobbler topping

175 g/6 oz self-raising flour, plus extra for dusting

2 level tsp baking powder

1/2 tsp ground turmeric

salt

3 tbsp butter

4–5 tbsp milk

golden chicken cobbler

Preheat the oven to 180°C/350°F/Gas Mark 4.

Put the flour in a bowl, season with salt and pepper, then add the chicken chunks and toss in the flour to coat. Melt the butter with the oil in a large flameproof casserole, add the chicken and cook, stirring, until the chicken is golden all over. Lift out with a slotted spoon, transfer to a plate and set aside.

Add the leek, spring onions and garlic to the casserole and cook over a medium heat, stirring, for 2 minutes until softened. Add the carrots and orange pepper to the pan and cook for another 2 minutes, then stir in the remaining seasoned flour, the tomato purée and the turmeric. Pour in the wine and stock, bring to the boil, then reduce the heat and cook over a low heat, stirring, until thickened. Return the chicken to the pan, add the bay leaf, cover, then bake in the preheated oven for 30 minutes.

Meanwhile, to make the cobbler topping, sift the flour, baking powder, turmeric and a pinch of salt into a large mixing bowl. Rub in the butter until the mixture resembles fine breadcrumbs, then stir in enough of the milk to make a smooth dough. Transfer to a clean, lightly floured board, knead lightly, then roll out to a thickness of about 1 cm/1/2 inch. Cut out rounds using a 5-cm/2-inch biscuit cutter.

Remove the casserole from the oven, remove and discard the bay leaf, and adjust the seasoning. Arrange the dough rounds over the top, then return to the oven and bake for another 30 minutes, or until the cobbler topping has risen and is lightly golden. Remove from the oven and serve hot.

serves 4

2 tbsp butter

2 large leeks, trimmed and sliced

150 g/5$\frac{1}{2}$ oz white mushrooms, sliced

2 courgettes, sliced

4 large tomatoes, peeled and chopped

1 tbsp chopped fresh dill

100 ml/3$\frac{1}{2}$ fl oz white wine

200 ml/7 fl oz fish stock

4 tsp cornflour

225 g/8 oz cod, cut into bite-sized chunks

225 g/8 oz haddock, cut into bite-sized chunks

salt and pepper

cobbler topping

175 g/6 oz self-raising flour, plus extra for dusting

2 level tsp baking powder

salt

1 tbsp chopped fresh dill

3 tbsp butter

4–5 tbsp milk

mixed fish cobbler with dill

Preheat the oven to 200°C/400°F/Gas Mark 6.

Melt the butter in a large flameproof casserole over a low heat. Add the leeks and cook, stirring, for 2 minutes until slightly softened. Add the mushrooms, courgettes, tomatoes and dill, and cook, stirring, for another 3 minutes.

Stir in the white wine and stock, bring to the boil, then reduce the heat to a simmer. Mix the cornflour with a little water to form a paste, then stir it into the casserole. Cook, stirring constantly, until thickened, then season with salt and pepper and remove from the heat.

To make the cobbler topping, sift the flour, baking powder and a pinch of salt into a large mixing bowl. Stir in the dill, then rub in the butter until the mixture resembles fine breadcrumbs. Stir in enough of the milk to make a smooth dough. Transfer to a clean, lightly floured board, knead lightly, then roll out to a thickness of about 1-cm/$\frac{1}{2}$-inch. Cut out rounds using a 5-cm/2-inch biscuit cutter.

Add the cod and haddock to the casserole and stir gently to mix. Arrange the dough rounds over the top, then return to the oven and bake for another 30 minutes, or until the cobbler topping has risen and is lightly golden. Remove from the oven and serve hot.

serves 4

1 tbsp olive oil

1 garlic clove, crushed

8 small onions, halved

2 celery sticks, sliced

225 g/8 oz swede, chopped

2 carrots, sliced

1/2 small cauliflower, broken into florets

225 g/8 oz mushrooms, sliced

400 g/14 oz can chopped tomatoes

55 g/2 oz red lentils

2 tbsp cornflour

3–4 tbsp water

300 ml/10 fl oz vegetable stock

2 tsp Tabasco sauce

oregano, plus extra sprigs to garnish

cobbler topping

225 g/8 oz self-raising flour

salt

4 tbsp butter

115 g/4 oz grated mature Cheddar cheese

2 tsp chopped fresh oregano

1 egg, lightly beaten

150 ml/5 fl oz milk

winter vegetable cobbler

Preheat oven to 180°C/350°F/Gas Mark 4.

Heat the oil and cook the garlic and onions for 5 minutes. Add the celery, swede, carrots and cauliflower, and cook for 2–3 minutes. Add the mushrooms, tomatoes and lentils. Mix the cornflour and water and stir into the pan with the stock, Tabasco and oregano.

Transfer to an ovenproof dish, cover and bake in the preheated oven for 20 minutes.

To make the cobbler topping, sift the flour with a pinch of salt into a bowl. Rub in the butter, then stir in most of the cheese and the chopped oregano. Beat the egg with the milk and add enough of the mixture to the dry ingredients to make a soft dough. Knead lightly, roll out to 1-cm/1/2-inch thick and cut into 5-cm/2-inch rounds.

Remove the dish from the oven and increase the temperature to 200°C/ 400°F/Gas Mark 6. Arrange the scones around the edge of the dish, brush with the remaining egg and milk and sprinkle with the reserved cheese. Cook for a further 10–12 minutes. Garnish with fresh oregano sprigs and serve.

serves 6–8

butter, for greasing

450 g/1 lb black cherries, stoned

25 g/1 oz golden granulated sugar

3 eggs

55 g/2 oz golden caster sugar

55 g/2 oz self-raising flour

2 tbsp cocoa powder

150 ml/5 fl oz double cream

300 ml/10 fl oz milk

2 tbsp kirsch (optional)

icing sugar, for dusting

light or heavy cream, to serve

cherry & chocolate clafoutis

Preheat the oven to 190°C/375°F/Gas Mark 5. Lightly butter a 23-cm/9-inch square ovenproof dish.

Arrange the cherries in the buttered dish, sprinkle with the granulated sugar and set aside.

Put the eggs and caster sugar in a bowl and whisk together until light and frothy. Sift the flour and cocoa powder onto a plate and add, all at once, to the egg mixture. Beat in thoroughly, then whisk in the cream followed by the milk and kirsch (if using). Pour the batter over the cherries.

Bake in the preheated oven for 50–60 minutes until slightly risen and set in the centre.

Sift icing sugar over the top and serve warm with cream.

serves 4

2 tbsp butter, plus extra for greasing

125 g/4^1/$_2$ oz caster sugar

3 eggs

60 g/2^1/$_4$ oz plain flour

250 ml/9 fl oz single cream

^{1}/$_2$ tsp ground cinnamon

450 g/1 lb blueberries

icing sugar, to decorate

single cream, to serve

blueberry clafoutis

Preheat the oven to 180°C/350°F/Gas Mark 4. Grease a
1-litre/1^3/$_4$-pint ovenproof dish with butter.

Put the remaining butter in a bowl with the sugar and whisk
together until fluffy. Add the eggs and beat together well. Mix
in the flour, then gradually stir in the cream followed by the
cinnamon. Continue to stir until smooth.

Arrange the blueberries in the bottom of the prepared dish, then
pour over the cream batter. Transfer to the preheated oven and
bake for about 30 minutes or until puffed and golden.

Remove from the oven, dust lightly with icing sugar and serve
with single cream.

serves 8

pastry

85 g/3 oz butter, cut into small pieces, plus extra for greasing

175 g/6 oz plain flour

1 tbsp water

1 egg, separated

filling

600 g/1 lb 5 oz prepared plums, rhubarb or gooseberries

60 g/2 1/4 oz soft light brown sugar

1 tbsp ground ginger

sugar lumps, crushed, for sprinkling

light or heavy cream, to serve

one-roll fruit pie

Grease a large baking sheet with a little butter and set aside until required.

To make the pastry, place the butter and flour in a mixing bowl and rub in the butter with the fingertips until the mixture resembles fine breadcrumbs. Add the water and work the mixture together until a soft dough has formed. Form into a ball. Wrap the dough and chill in the refrigerator for 30 minutes.

Preheat the oven to 200°C/400°F/Gas Mark 6.

Roll out the chilled pastry to a round about 35 cm/14 inches in diameter. Transfer the pastry circle to the centre of the prepared baking sheet. Lightly beat the egg yolk, then brush the pastry with it. To make the filling, mix the plums (or other fruit) with the brown sugar and ground ginger. Pile it into the centre of the pastry.

Turn in the edges of the circle of pastry all the way around. Lightly beat the egg white, then brush the surface of the pastry with it and sprinkle with the crushed sugar lumps.

Bake in the preheated oven for 35 minutes, or until golden brown. Serve warm.

4

Nice 'n' Spicy

serves 4

10 firm but ripe apricots,

25 g/1 oz demerara sugar

½ tsp ground ginger

1 tbsp orange juice

grated zest of 1 orange

1 tbsp orange-flavoured
liqueur, such as Cointreau

crumble topping

115 g/4 oz self-raising flour

$^1/_2$ tsp ground ginger

100 g/3$^1/_2$ oz unsalted butter,
diced

5 tbsp demerara sugar

50 g/1$^3/_4$ oz pistachio nuts,
finely chopped

chopped pistachio nuts,
to decorate

double cream, to serve

apricot & ginger crumble with orange liqueur

Preheat the oven to 200°C/400°F/Gas Mark 6.

Stone the apricots, then cut them in half. Put them in the bottom of an ovenproof pie dish, sprinkle over the sugar, ginger, orange juice and zest, and the orange-flavoured liqueur, then cook in the preheated oven for 5–10 minutes until heated through.

Meanwhile, to make the crumble topping, put the flour and ginger in a bowl, then use your fingertips to rub in the unsalted butter until crumbly. Then stir in 4 tablespoons of the demerara sugar and the pistachio nuts. Lightly sprinkle the crumble mixture over the fruit in an even layer. Do not press the crumble into the fruit or it will become mushy. Sprinkle over the remaining demerara sugar and decorate with chopped pistachio nuts.

Bake in the preheated oven for 25–30 minutes or until the crumble topping is golden brown. Serve hot with double cream decorated with chopped pistachio nuts.

serves 4

225 g/8 oz raisins

225 g/8 oz dried figs, chopped

700 ml/1¼ pints water

3 tbsp demerara sugar

grated zest and juice of
1 orange

½ tsp ground cloves,
or to taste

crumble topping

185 g/6½ oz plain flour

55 g/2 oz demerara sugar,
plus extra for sprinkling

100 g/3½ oz unsalted butter,
melted

50 g/1¾ oz hazelnuts,
chopped

vanilla or orange-flavoured
ice cream, to serve

sweet fig & raisin crumble

Put the raisins and figs in a large bowl, cover with the water and leave to soak overnight or for at least 8 hours.

Preheat the oven to 180°C/350°F/Gas Mark 4.

Drain the figs and raisins, reserving the soaking liquid. Put the fruit in a large saucepan with the sugar and 600 ml/1 pint of the soaking liquid. Bring to the boil, then reduce the heat and simmer for about 10 minutes, or until the fruit has softened.

Meanwhile, to make the crumble topping, put the flour and demerara sugar in a large bowl, then mix in half the melted butter. Stir in the chopped nuts, then quickly mix in the remaining butter until crumbly.

Remove the fruit from the heat, stir in the orange zest and juice, and the ground cloves, then carefully pour the mixture into an ovenproof pie dish. Carefully arrange the crumble over the fruit in an even layer – keep your touch light or the crumble will sink into the filling and go mushy. Scatter a little more sugar over the top, then transfer to the preheated oven and bake for 25 minutes, or until the crumble topping is golden brown.

Serve hot with vanilla or orange-flavoured ice cream.

serves 4

225 g/8 oz prunes, chopped

225 g/8 oz golden raisins (sultanas)

700 ml/1¼ pints water

3 tbsp demerara sugar

1 tsp mixed spice

1 tbsp dark rum (optional)

crumble topping

115 g/4 oz self-raising flour

½ tsp mixed spice

100 g/3½ oz unsalted butter, diced

5 tbsp demerara sugar

crème fraîche, to serve

prune & golden raisin crumble with mixed spices

Put the prunes and sultanas in a large bowl, cover with the water and leave to soak overnight or for at least 8 hours.

Preheat the oven to 180°C/350°F/Gas Mark 4.

Drain the fruit, reserving the soaking liquid. Put the fruit in a large saucepan with the sugar and 600 ml/1 pint of the soaking liquid. Bring to the boil, then reduce the heat and simmer for about 10 minutes, or until the fruit has softened.

Meanwhile, to make the crumble topping, put the flour and mixed spice in a bowl, then use your fingertips to rub in the butter until crumbly. Stir in 4 tablespoons of the demerara sugar.

Remove the fruit from the heat, stir in the mixed spice, and the rum, if using, then pour into an ovenproof pie dish. Carefully arrange the crumble over the fruit in an even layer – keep your touch light or the crumble will sink into the filling and go mushy. Scatter the remaining sugar over the top, then transfer to the preheated oven and bake for 25 minutes, or until the crumble topping is golden brown.

Serve hot with crème fraîche.

serves 4

8 firm but ripe plums

25 g/1 oz demerara sugar

½ tsp ground ginger

grated zest of 1 lemon

crumble topping

185 g/6 ½oz plain flour

$^1/_2$ tsp ground ginger

55 g/2 oz demerara sugar,
plus extra for sprinkling

100 g/3$^1/_2$ oz unsalted butter,
melted

warm custard, to serve

pieces of stem ginger,
to decorate

plum crumble with lemon & ginger

Preheat the oven to 200°C/400°F/Gas Mark 6.

Using a sharp knife, halve the plums, remove and discard the stones, then cut the flesh into fairly thick slices. Arrange the plum slices in an ovenproof pie dish, sprinkle over the sugar, ground ginger and lemon zest, then cook in the preheated oven for 5–10 minutes until heated through.

To make the crumble topping, put the flour, ground ginger and demerara sugar in a large bowl, then mix in the melted butter until crumbly.

Carefully arrange the crumble over the plums in an even layer – keep your touch light or the crumble will sink into the filling and go mushy. Scatter a little more sugar over the top, then transfer to the preheated oven and bake for 25–30 minutes, or until the crumble topping is golden brown.

Serve with warm custard and decorated with pieces of stem ginger.

serves 4

6 large, firm peaches

55 g/2 oz unsalted butter

$^1/_2$ tsp ground star anise

25 g/1 oz caster sugar

125 ml/4 fl oz water

2 tbsp kirsch

crumble topping

115 g/4 oz self-raising flour

$^1/_2$ tsp ground cinnamon

100 g/3$^1/_2$ oz unsalted butter, diced

5 tbsp demerara sugar

50 g/1$^3/_4$ oz cashew nuts, finely chopped

vanilla or peach-flavoured ice cream, to serve

roasted peach crumble with star anise

Preheat the oven to 190°C/375°F/Gas Mark 5.

Using a sharp knife, halve the peaches and remove the stones. Bring a pan of water to the boil, add the peach halves, then cook for about 3 minutes until the skins are wrinkled. Remove from the heat, lift out the peaches and leave to cool slightly.

Melt the unsalted butter in a small saucepan, add the star anise and cook, stirring for 30 seconds. Add the caster sugar and the water and cook gently, stirring, until beginning to caramelize. Stir in the kirsch, then remove from the heat.

To make the crumble topping, put the flour and cinnamon in a bowl, then use your fingertips to rub in the unsalted butter until crumbly. Then stir in 4 tablespoons of the demerara sugar and the chopped cashew nuts.

When the peaches are cool enough to handle (use a knife and fork if necessary), gently remove and discard the skins. Cut the peach flesh into bite-sized chunks and arrange evenly in the bottom of an ovenproof pie dish. Pour over the syrup, then lightly sprinkle over the crumble mixture in an even layer. Do not press the crumble into the syrup or it will become mushy. Sprinkle over the remaining demerara sugar and bake in the preheated oven for 25–30 minutes, or until the crumble topping is golden brown.

Serve hot with vanilla or peach-flavoured ice cream.

serves 4

350 g/12 oz cherries, stoned

$^1/_2$ tsp allspice

40 g/1$^1/_2$ oz demerara sugar

3 tbsp cherry brandy

crumble topping

185 g/6$^1/_2$ oz plain flour

$^1/_2$ tsp ground allspice

55 g/2 oz demerara sugar,
plus extra for sprinkling

100 g/3$^1/_2$ oz unsalted butter,
melted

50 g/1$^3/_4$ oz almonds,
chopped

vanilla ice cream, to serve

spiced cherry crumble

Preheat the oven to 190°C/375°F/Gas Mark 5.

Put the cherries, allspice, demerara sugar and cherry brandy into a saucepan and stir gently over a low heat for 3 minutes. Transfer the cherries and juices to an ovenproof pie dish.

To make the crumble topping, put the flour, allspice and demerara sugar in a large bowl, then mix in half the melted butter. Stir in the chopped nuts, then quickly mix in the remaining butter until crumbly.

Carefully arrange the crumble over the cherries in an even layer – keep your touch light or the crumble will sink into the filling and go mushy. Scatter a little more sugar over the top, then transfer to the preheated oven and bake for 15–20 minutes, or until the crumble topping is golden brown.

Serve hot with vanilla ice cream.

serves 4

800 g/1 lb 12 oz ripe but firm gooseberries

2 tbsp honey

50 g/1¾ oz caster sugar, or to taste

cobbler topping

200 g/7 oz self-raising flour, plus extra for dusting

pinch of salt

½ tsp mixed spice

3 tbsp unsalted butter

2 tbsp caster sugar

1 egg, beaten

about 5 tbsp milk, plus extra for glazing

vanilla ice cream, to serve

gooseberry cobbler with honey & mixed spice

Preheat the oven to 200°C/400°F/Gas Mark 6.

Top and tail the gooseberries. Arrange them evenly in the bottom of an ovenproof dish, then sprinkle over the honey and sugar and cook in the preheated oven for 5–10 minutes until heated through.

To make the cobbler topping, sift the flour, salt and mixed spice into a large mixing bowl. Rub in the unsalted butter until the mixture resembles fine breadcrumbs, then mix in the sugar, followed by the beaten egg. Stir in enough of the milk to make a smooth dough. Transfer to a clean, lightly floured board, knead lightly, then roll out to a thickness of about 1 cm/½ inch. Cut out rounds using a 5-cm/2-inch biscuit cutter. Arrange the dough rounds over the gooseberries, then brush the tops with a little milk.

Bake in the preheated oven for 25–30 minutes, or until the cobbler topping has risen and is lightly golden.

Serve hot with vanilla ice cream.

serves 4

2 ripe mangoes, stoned and
cut into fairly thick slices

250 g/9 oz blueberries

½ tsp nutmeg

1 tbsp lime juice

50 g/1¾ oz caster sugar,
or to taste

cobbler topping

200 g/7 oz self-raising flour,
plus extra for dusting

pinch of salt

½ tsp cinnamon

3 tbsp unsalted butter

2 tbsp caster sugar

3 tbsp dried blueberries
(optional)

1 egg, beaten

about 5 tbsp milk, plus extra
for glazing

warm custard, to serve

spiced mango & blueberry cobbler

Preheat the oven to 200°C/400°F/Gas Mark 6.

Put the mango slices and blueberries in the bottom of an ovenproof dish, then sprinkle over the nutmeg, lime juice and caster sugar. Cook in the preheated oven for 5–10 minutes until heated through.

To make the cobbler topping, sift the flour, salt and cinnamon into a large mixing bowl. Rub in the unsalted butter until the mixture resembles fine breadcrumbs, then mix in the sugar, and the dried blueberries, if using. Add the beaten egg, then stir in enough of the milk to make a smooth dough. Transfer to a clean, lightly floured board, knead lightly, then roll out to a thickness of about 1 cm/½ inch. Cut out rounds using a 5-cm/2-inch biscuit cutter. Arrange the dough rounds over the fruit, then brush the tops with a little milk.

Bake in the preheated oven for 25–30 minutes, or until the cobbler topping has risen and is lightly golden.

Serve hot with warm custard.

serves 4

1 large onion, peeled and sliced

2 courgettes, sliced

85 g/3 oz mushrooms, sliced

2 large carrots, roughly chopped

225 g/8 oz black-eyed beans

175 g/6 oz haricot beans

400 g/14 oz canned tomatoes

1 tsp mild chilli powder

salt and pepper

cobbler topping

175 g/6 oz self-raising flour, plus extra for dusting

2 level tsp baking powder

1/2 tsp paprika

salt

3 tbsp unsalted butter

4–5 tbsp milk

spicy vegetable cobbler

Preheat the oven to 200°C/400°F/Gas Mark 6.

Put the onion, courgettes, mushrooms, carrots, black-eyed beans, haricot beans and canned tomatoes in a casserole. Sprinkle over the chilli powder and season to taste with salt and pepper. Transfer to the preheated oven and bake for 15 minutes.

Meanwhile, to make the cobbler topping, sift the flour, baking powder, paprika and a pinch of salt into a large mixing bowl. Rub in the unsalted butter until the mixture resembles fine breadcrumbs, then stir in enough of the milk to make a smooth dough. Transfer to a clean, lightly floured board, knead lightly, then roll out to a thickness of about 1 cm/1/2 inch. Cut out rounds using a 5-cm/2-inch biscuit cutter.

Remove the casserole from the oven, arrange the dough rounds over the top, then return to the oven and bake for 30 minutes, or until the cobbler topping has risen and is lightly golden.

Serve hot.

serves 4

2 tbsp plain flour

900 g/2 lb stewing beef, cut into bite-sized chunks

2 tbsp chilli oil or olive oil

1 large onion, peeled and sliced

1 garlic clove, crushed

1 small red chilli, deseeded and chopped

1 courgette, sliced

1 red pepper, deseeded and cut into small chunks

150 g/5½ oz mushrooms, sliced

1 tbsp tomato purée

500 ml/18 fl oz red wine

250 ml/9 fl oz beef stock or vegetable stock

1 bay leaf

salt and pepper

cobbler topping

175 g/6 oz self-raising flour, plus extra for dusting

2 level tsp baking powder

pinch of cayenne pepper

salt

3 tbsp butter

4–5 tbsp milk

beef cobbler with chilli

Preheat the oven to 160°C/325°F/Gas Mark 3.

Put the flour in a bowl, season with salt and pepper, then add the beef chunks and toss in the flour to coat. Heat half of the oil in a large flameproof casserole. Add the beef and cook, stirring, until the meat has browned all over and is sealed. Lift out with a slotted spoon, transfer to a plate and set aside.

Heat the remaining oil in the casserole, add the onion and garlic and cook over a medium heat, stirring, for 2 minutes until softened. Add the chilli, courgette, red pepper and mushrooms and cook, stirring, for another 3 minutes.

Stir in the remaining seasoned flour and the tomato purée, then stir in the red wine, scraping the bottom gently to deglaze the pan. Pour in the stock, add the bay leaf, then bring to the boil. Reduce the heat and cook over a low heat, stirring, until thickened. Return the beef to the pan, cover and bake in the preheated oven for 45 minutes.

Meanwhile, to make the cobbler topping, sift the flour, baking powder, cayenne pepper and a pinch of salt into a large mixing bowl. Rub in the butter until the mixture resembles fine breadcrumbs, then stir in enough of the milk to make a smooth dough. Transfer to a clean, lightly floured board, knead lightly, then roll out to a thickness of about 1 cm/½ inch. Cut out rounds using a 5-cm/2-inch biscuit cutter.

Remove the casserole from the oven, remove and discard the bay leaf, and adjust the seasoning to taste. Arrange the dough rounds over the top, then return to the oven and bake for another 30 minutes, or until the cobbler topping has risen and is lightly golden. Serve hot.